THE PRAYER CHAIN

A Christmas Story about Prayer.

KIMBERLY WILLIAMS SHAW

ILLUSTRATED BY RICHARD STERGULZ

A Faith Parenting Guide can be found on page 32.

Faith Kids™ is an imprint of
Cook Communications Ministries, Colorado Springs, CO 80918
Cook Communications, Paris, Ontario
Kingsway Communications, Eastbourne, England

THE PRAYER CHAIN

Published in association with the literary agency of Janet Kobobel Grant, Books & Such,
3093 Maiden Lane, Altadena, CA 91001.

Edited by Marianne Hering
Designed by Matthew Doherty

First printing, 2000
Printed in Singapore
04 03 02 01 00   5 4 3 2 1

Dedicated to:

Mark, my husband and best friend,

and God, my life and inspiration.

Do not be anxious about anything,

but in everything, by prayer and petition,

with thanksgiving,

present your requests to God.

Philippians 4:6

CHRISTMAS. TOMORROW'S CHRISTMAS! thought eight-year-old Jessie as she stared at the shiny package beneath the Christmas tree. *What's inside?* she wondered. Could she wait until morning to open it? She grabbed the small gift and snuggled beneath her blanket.

The fire crackled. The old ranch house provided no other heat. Jessie watched the last piece of wood burn to ash. *Momma will find some wood*, she told herself, trying to chase away her fears. But her numb fingers and toes reminded her that this would not be a normal, gentle winter.

T he phone rang. Jessie jumped up and ran to the kitchen.

"Hello," Jessie answered with her most polite phone voice, the gift still cradled in her arms.

"Good morning, Jessie!" the voice said. "This is Mrs. Livingston. Is your mother around? The prayer chain has another answered prayer."

Momma's name was on a list with eleven other women from the church. Mrs. Livingston's job was to call Momma and ask her to pray. Momma's job was to call Mrs. Moses and ask her to pray. And Mrs. Moses's job was to call the next person, and so on, until a chain of twelve women were praying together.

Jessie's eyes widened. *Another answered prayer!* Forgetting her phone manners, Jessie yelled into the mouthpiece, "Momma, it's the prayer chain."

Momma's footsteps echoed on the back porch. She walked through the room carrying a small bundle of branches. A blast of cold air brushed past Jessie's cheeks. Momma placed the kindling on the brick hearth and smiled. Jessie tried to return the smile but couldn't take her eyes off the handful of branches.

Is that all there is, Momma? Jessie thought. *It's going to be a cold Christmas.*

J essie returned to the tree.
Homemade sugar cookies dangled from its
otherwise bare branches. Even the
thought of biting into a cookie
couldn't take the worry
from her heart.

Jessie listened as
Momma spoke to Mrs.
Livingston. "God is so
good!" said Momma
into the phone. "That's
wonderful news."

Jessie knew she wasn't
supposed to eavesdrop, but
she couldn't help herself. She peeked
under the wrapping paper hoping
Momma wouldn't notice she was hearing
every word.

Momma called Mrs. Moses, the next person on the prayer chain. When she was finished, she walked into her bedroom. Jessie followed, the gift secure in her arms. She fell to her knees beside Momma, who had knelt to pray. Jessie listened as her mother thanked God for another answered prayer.

"Thank You for healing that little boy, Lord," Momma said aloud.

Patiently Jessie waited as Momma then prayed about the unanswered requests.

"Momma," Jessie said, "which prayer was answered now?"

"Barbara's son, Tommy, isn't sick anymore. The doctors said they can't find anything wrong with him."

Jessie smiled. Tommy had been in the hospital, but God had answered the prayer and healed him. "Can I write it down now, Momma?" Jessie ran to the kitchen, leaving the gift behind on the bed.

In the kitchen sat a glass jar that was filled with thin strips of white paper. Written on each piece of paper was an answer to prayer. Since the beginning of the year, the women in the telephone chain prayed every day for those in need.

Momma laughed and said, "I don't know if any more slips will fit into that jar, sweetheart. We may need to get another."

Jessie hugged the jar tight and laughed with her mother. In her arms were the answers to dozens of prayers. She wrote the newly answered prayer on a strip of paper and placed it inside the jar.

Job for Mr. Sutton

Tommy is well

That evening Jessie jumped up and down as she stared out the window.

"Look, Momma, it's snowing!" she said, pressing her nose against the icy pane. "Tomorrow I'll build a snowman."

Building a snowman means cold fingers and toes, she thought. She looked at the small pile of branches and shivered.

"We'll need more wood for Christmas morning," she said to Momma.

Mother stood next to Jessie and pulled her close.

"Momma." Jessie's eyes filled with tears. "We're going to be so cold."

I wish Daddy were here, thought Jessie. But he went to live with Jesus when she was just a baby.

"Don't cry, Jessie," said Momma. "God knows our needs. He will take care of us."

Together they watched the tiny snowflakes fall to the ground.

Momma grabbed Jessie's hands. "Let's pray."

Jessie squeezed her eyes so tight she saw spots. Her forehead wrinkled.

"God, please help us get more wood. It's really cold down here!" Jessie wanted so much to believe God had heard her prayer.

She looked at the jar full of answered prayers. A tiny bubble of hope formed in her heart. *Will You do the same for us, God?* she wondered. *Do You care?*

J essie awoke
Christmas morning
to find the earth
covered with snow.

She ran and threw open the
front door. Surprised, she yelled,
"Momma, come here!"

 Mother hurried to the door.

 "Look! It's a mountain of wood,"
Jessie shouted, jumping on tiptoe.
 "It's enough wood for months!"

 "For a few
weeks, anyhow,"
Momma laughed.

A ring of colored paper circled the doorknob. It read, "God Bless You."

Jessie looked up at her mother. "Oh, Momma, you were right. God does care."

Jessie took the note from the doorknob while Momma built a fire. She started to break open the ring to place it inside the jar when a thought came to her. Quickly she ran to her room and dug inside her desk drawer.

She returned with a bottle of glue. Taking one of the answered prayers from the jar, Jessie looped it inside the colorful ring and glued it closed, forming another ring. Then she grabbed and looped another and another until a long chain fell to the floor.

"Jessie, what are you doing?" Mother asked as she walked into the kitchen. Jessie's feet were buried beneath the paper chain. "What are you making with all the answered prayers?"

"A prayer chain." Jessie beamed, her hands covered with glue. "It's to wrap around our Christmas tree!"

Momma smiled. "What a wonderful idea." She grabbed a slip of paper with an answered prayer and helped Jessie loop every one within another until the jar was empty.

"Can I wrap it around our tree, Momma? Can I?"

"Of course!" Momma answered.

Mother started at the top, looping the newest answer around the highest point of the tree. The words "God Bless You" shone brighter than any store-bought star could ever shine. On tiptoe, Jessie circled the tree, laying the chain on each branch.

"Oh, Momma, isn't our tree beautiful?" Jessie said. She had completely forgotten about her present still in Momma's room.

She touched the chain of answered prayers. "Let's pray and thank God for the wood and the gifts He has given us all year."

Jessie grabbed her mother's hands. They bowed their heads.

The phone rang.

Jessie and her mother looked at each other and smiled. Mother grabbed a slip of paper and a pencil.

"Hello," Jessie answered with her most polite phone voice.

CREATE YOUR OWN PRAYER CHAIN

Would you like to make your own prayer chain
like Jessie's? Here's how to start:

You'll need:
- glue or a stapler
- pencils and crayons or markers
- scissors
- friends and family members
  to add some fun
- construction paper or plain white paper

Find the marked sheet at the end of this
book. Remove the sheet of paper
by gently tearing it along
the perforation.

Cut each strip with a scissors as marked. Write a prayer request on each slip of paper. If you want, decorate the slips by coloring them with markers or crayons. Glue or staple one request into a loop.

Attach the next paper by looping it through the first loop. Staple or glue it closed. Continue until all the requests are looped together in a chain. If you have more requests, make extra slips using your own paper. Cut rectangles 1 inch by 10 to 10 inches.

Hang the chain in a visible area like the kitchen or dining area. Make sure it is in a place that your child can easily reach. As a family, pray for the requests written on each loop. Then wait.

Every time God answers a request (like Grandma gets out of the hospital or your neighbor comes with you to church), attach an extra loop to that link in the chain. Make sure the added loop is a different color so it is easy to see. Decorate that special loop with stars and bright colors. Whenever you see the paper chain, thank God for being faithful to answer our prayers.

For the eyes of the Lord are on the righteous
and his ears are attentive to their prayer.

1 Peter 3:12

THE PRAYER CHAIN

AGE: 4 to 7 years

LIFE ISSUE
My child needs to understand that prayer
is a wonderful way to talk to God.

SPIRITUAL BUILDING BLOCK
Prayer

LEARNING STYLES

Sight: Look for pictures in magazines that show things your family is thankful for. You can also gather photos of friends and family members. Using glue and construction paper make a "collage of thanks" out of the materials. Hang it up in your child's room so it can serve as a visual reminder that God blesses him or her with good things. At your next family prayer time, thank God for some of the things from the collage.

Sound: Read the Lord's prayer from Matthew 6:9-13. Ask your child questions to make sure he or she understands each verse. (Hint: "hallowed" means holy, consecrated, sacred and revered.) At your evening prayer time, ask your child to pray his or her own personal version of one verse.

Touch: With your child, make a list of all the places he or she can pray. After listing all the usual spots, add these places mentioned in the Bible: Jesus praying on a mountain (Mark 6:46) and standing in a river (Luke 3:21-22). Jonah prayed in the belly of a fish (Jonah 2:1)! Find a different place to pray every day this next week (while taking a walk, playing at the park, riding in the car, etc.). Have your child draw pictures of himself or herself in prayer at those places. Pin these up around the home to celebrate the truth that your child can talk to God anywhere and anytime.

"You may ask me for anything in my name, and I will do it."
John 14:14